RARE SENSE
One Day It Will Be Common!

A Practical Guide to a
Fulfilled and Balanced Life

 www.trafford.com

North America & international
toll-free: 1 888 232 4444 (USA & Canada)
phone: 250 383 6864 ♦ fax: 250 383 6804 ♦ email: info@trafford.com

The United Kingdom & Europe
phone: +44 (0)1865 722 113 ♦ local rate: 0845 230 9601
facsimile: +44 (0)1865 722 868 ♦ email: info.uk@trafford.com

10 9 8 7 6 5 4 3 2

This book is dedicated to my mom, Eleanor, my wife Tammy and my daughter Melinda. Three females who have had a profound impact on my life and always help me to be the best man, son, husband and father that I can be.

ACKNOWLEDGMENTS

Thus far in this lifetime there have been so many people who have helped me, inspired me and encouraged me that it would be impossible to mention all of them here. For that I am truly blessed. However, there are some people I would especially like to thank: Eleanor Shade (my mother), Tammy Shade (my wife), Melinda Shade (my daughter), John Shade (my brother), Cyndi Hogue, (my sister), Harry L. Shade, (my father), Don Kinel, Rick Weinard, Debbie Hohman, Reverend Myrl Gephardt, Father Karl Kish, Mike Serotko, John Myers Jr., Gene Zorn, and Emmet Adams.

CONTENTS

My Story
Preface

Rare Sense Principles

MY STORY

Oh, where do I begin? First of all, I do not have a Ph.D. in anything. I am not a doctor, lawyer, clergyman, psychologist or master guru. I am a somewhat normal, everyday guy, with what I believe is the ability to see things from a RARE SENSE perspective. Ever since I can remember, I have always looked at the world a little differently than other people. I have never thought of myself as better than others; actually quite the contrary, I sometimes felt inferior to others who seemed to be really comfortable with the ways of the world. I often thought there must be something wrong with me. I just did not seem to get it!

To that end, I began searching for the answers outside of me. I asked the tough questions of my boyhood pastor, Reverend Myrl Gephart, and a priest, Father Karl Kish, from St. Joseph's Catholic Church in my hometown of Newton Falls, Ohio. I especially bugged my mother with question after question. Fortunately for me, they turned out to be very patient and understanding and they were the first to teach me to look for the answers inside myself, since the answers I was seeking could not either be found in any particular book, building or, quite frankly, outside of me at all. The answers were in my soul.

I have come to love and respect anyone who uses their God given abilities. I am working on it and growing ever more spiritual everyday. You probably noticed I said spiritual and not religious. That's because I believe that being spiritual supersedes being religious.

There I go again, seeing things a little bit differently. And that is what this book is all about. Looking at things from a spiritual or RARE SENSE perspective, rather than any other way.

Hopefully, I will either be able to touch a few lives with the material in this book, or at the very least get some others thinking a little bit differently and saying "ah ha".

I really believe that is what our world needs today. We need the different thinkers to continue to exert themselves even more. Maybe you have noticed all the books lately concerning spirituality.

Do you think that is an accident? Hardly! We as a human race are at a crossroads. We can either change our world or perish with it! Now, this is not going to be some gloom and doom book, merely a different way of looking at things! I admit it, I have read and/or listened to audio versions of many spiritual books over the past 30 plus years and I truly believe that my spirit guides are helping me write this one.

Remember these are my thoughts and ideas on things, some perhaps original, though I doubt very many of them. Since we are all one and all come from God, we actually all have helped to write this book. Some thoughts and ideas are ones that I read and/or heard elsewhere and are simply sharing with you in my own way. You can call me crazy; I will accept that because being "crazy" keeps me from going insane! To talk about spirituality you have to actually be out of your mind!

Now like Walsch, Chopra and others like them, I know I am going to ruffle some feathers and downright tick some people off. Some may even call for my head. But that is OK, because they are exercising their Free Will by doing so. All I ask is that everyone that reads this book, do so with an open mind. I am not trying to change anyone's religious beliefs, just perhaps get you to look at things a little bit differently. In the end, if you read this book and say that guy is crazy or a blasphemer or worse, great, at least you exposed yourself to some different ideas.

However, if you are the type of person that sees the world differently than others, I hope this book helps confirm that there are others like you out there and inspire you to continue to approach things from a perspective of RARE SENSE. If you are the conventional type of person who sees things from a position of common sense, I hope this book can start you on a journey of incredible discovery and enlightenment.

Before I close I just want to say that my biggest hope is that this book will touch a lot of lives in a very special way. You see, I am on a spiritual journey also and I believe that writing this book is something I need to do to help me along my way.

Love and light to you all!
Harry Shade

PREFACE

What is Rare Sense? It is a knowing deep in our soul as to whom we really are; spiritual beings in human form. It is an understanding that there is a higher intelligence at work in the universe and that everything in the universe is perfect. There are no coincidences, we are creating everything. Every moment of every single day we have the power to create our world anew. We choose how our life is going to go and how we are going to deal with its inevitable ups and downs.

There is a lesson or experience in everything that has happened to us and is going to happen to us. The main point of it all I believe is to be thankful for everything in the world, the good and the bad, the ups and the downs, the left and the right, for it is all part of life. We should live each and every moment like it is our last on this earth for we do not know how long we will be here. What is most important is not material things, but love. We are all equal in the eyes of the universe, no one person better than another, no one person more important than another. We need this planet to survive in this human form and we also need each other. We are all going back to the same place once we leave earth.

People with RARE SENSE do not need laws, commandments or any thing else for us to understand that we should be good to each other, that we should not kill, covet thy neighbors wife, etc.

We find such things to be highly redundant and totally unnecessary. We look at the world and see all the possibilities for good and love. We do not judge others but we do speak the truth. We know what does and what does not work and try to live our lives as a testament to the innate perfection of the universe. We see the good in everyone and know that because we are spiritual beings, in other words God experiencing itself, that we are inherently good, not evil. We are essentially pure love expressed. We seek to improve ourselves, thus improving our world in the process.

We do not try to control others. We do not use guilt to get what we want. We do not want power over others but power with others. We know that giving and receiving are equally important for we need both givers and receivers! We try to approach everything from a position of love.

Since we are in human form, we are not perfect and we are not striving for perfection. We simply want to experience all that life has to offer. We are messengers for the universe. Our message is a simple one; love is all there is and all there ever needs to be. We need nothing to be happy, we simply are happy. People with rare sense are the perpetually positive people. Our glasses are always half full and every moment of every day brings new possibilities. We are the "morning" people that seem to drive some people crazy. We are literally out of our minds, because it is truly in this state that we can experience it all.

Is it something we are born with? Absolutely! Everyone is born with rare sense and some of us recognize it right away. Quite frankly, it took almost 25 years for me to understand and recognize it in myself. All of us come to this lifetime with a purpose. All of us have known the young child who seemed to be wiser than his/her age. We call them "old souls" yet even old souls are child-like because children are dreamers and think nothing is impossible. It is only when we grow up that we sometimes lose that inner child.

Well, we actually never lose our inner child; we just bury it under a pile of emotional crap. Things like guilt, fear, jealously, depression and anxiety. Some of us come to a place of peace and contentment when we are about to leave this earth and transition back into the spirit realm. Some of us will not get to that point of clarity in this lifetime and that's O.K. We are all on our own path, our own journey.

But those of us that have come to that point of clarity in this lifetime, those that have rare sense are all messengers. We are here to tell the world that we can have it all. There is enough of everything for everyone. There is enough money, enough food, enough air, enough water, simply enough of everything. We just need to remember who we are, where we come from and it will all be very clear to us.

OK, Harry, how do you know all of this? The only way I can describe it is when you fall in love with someone and you just know, at least at that point, that they are the one for you. It is a feeling deep down inside. It does not come from your head or ego; it actually resonates deep in your soul. Like the first time I looked deeply into Tammy's eyes. My heart nearly leapt out of my chest because I knew that I had found my soul mate. The person I would spend the rest of my earthly time with during this lifetime. There was such a feeling of calm and peace in that moment.

I carry that calm and peace with me every day. Again, as I have stated before, I am in human form so I am not perfect, at least not now, not here. But I come from perfection, for the universe is in fact perfect. God is perfection because God is the universe, the force that gave us life.

What does it mean to have Rare Sense? Lama Sura Das describes us as "seekers". People with rare sense are actively seeking to improve themselves spiritually. We know that for every answer we get about life and how it is supposed to work we will also continue to have questions. We know that we will never stop growing, never stop learning and will always seek the truth.

I am a Spiritualist and as a Spiritualist I am not trying to convert anyone to anything. I want people to find their own path to their truth during this lifetime. I am simply trying to provide guidance, a road map for higher spiritual enlightenment. I am still learning things, experiencing things in an effort to be the best person I can be, as are all people who recognize that they are on a spiritual path. And the truth is we are all spiritual. Some of us feel we need the warmth, guidance, control and belonging of a religion. Some of those people may someday find out that all they need is within them. Until then I wish them well on their spiritual journey.

Some of us know that we really do not need anything, that all we need is in fact inside us and that we control our lives through the choices we make.

No matter where we are in our search, in reality we are all seeking to be more spiritual, since we are all just trying to remember who we really are.

Writing this book and sharing my thoughts on this matter are part of my spiritual journey. I decided that I should share my thoughts because I do not have a doctorate in religion and I did not study for 12 years in a monastery. Even though those things have worked for others, I am trying to tell the common folk that they can find their spirituality without having to do all those things normally considered necessary with becoming enlightened. We can all get to wherever we want to go on our own. This book is perhaps just another guide.

The Principles of Rare Sense

Chapter 1: **Know**

"Know, first, who you are,
and then adorn yourself
accordingly." - Epictetus

As you develop your rare sense you will notice a natural transition from Hope to Belief to Knowing.

When we first start on this spiritual adventure we have hope for the future, hope that we can find our way and hope that we can accomplish the journey.

Hope is actually a cry for help, a pleading to the universe. Hope still allows the ego quite a bit of control. There is still the need to judge others but more importantly to judge ourselves. We still feel that we need physical possessions to be whole. We are still not quite convinced that there is an abundance of everything. We are still not convinced that we do not need anything even though the universe will always supply all that we need. Holding on to material things is important because it is things that give us the most security. We say things like "I hope I can make it through the day."
"I hope I can pay the bills this month!" I hope, I hope. I hope! There is a certain amount of desperation in hope.

However, it is through hope that we reach the next level of belief. It is through hope that great things are accomplished! All things begin with hope because without hope we cannot move on to the next level. Without hope, nothing else would happen because hope is what gets us to ask for help from the universe. In most cases it is what gets us to pray. It leads directly to the next level.

Then slowly, usually imperceptibly; hope grows into belief. We now believe in what we do and say. We believe in the future, we believe we can find our way, we believe in ourselves and others. We believe we can accomplish things. Our confidence grows. We have more conviction and more clarity. We can feel it inside! Doubt is being removed more and more, little by little. Things become easier. We are finding it less necessary or desirable to judge ourselves or others. Things that seemed so important just yesterday are starting to take on a less ominous role in our lives. A great book that I would recommend about believing is entitled "I'll see it when I believe it!" by Wayne Dyer. The old adage is I'll believe it when I see it but as Wayne Dyer so wonderfully puts it, we have to believe in it before we can ever truly see it. That's the way the universe works.

Next, we come into knowing and when we reach this level the whole universe opens up to us. We say "Aha" a lot! Nothing is impossible. We have a total sense of peace & well being. It is quite clear who we really are, a spiritual being in human form. We now live for the moment and make a life instead of a living. We know that we are responsible for all of it. We are creating life anew, every moment of every day. We know that we make the choices that control our destiny. We are our future.

We understand the perfection of it all, how everything is inter-connected, interdependent, and inseparable. In other words it is all one within itself. There is no separation. Everything is a necessary part of the whole and that whole is God expressing itself.

There is no longer a need to judge because we are simply judging ourselves. Life is all of it, the ups, the downs, the good, the bad, the highs and the lows. And we are creating all of it and we are a part of it at the same time.

Even at this stage of knowing, we are still in human form. We also understand that we have a lot more to learn and experience. The ego still tries in vain to exert some influence and from time to time succeeds, if for no other reason than to constantly remind us who we really are. These times come fewer and fewer between. For some they disappear altogether and for others they are always there in some shape or manner. But we will notice them less and less. We will not give those moments anymore of our time and effort than we know they deserve, which is no time at all.

We are not perfect when we are in human form! We know that, so perfection is not the goal here. The goal is to live life to the fullest, knowing that when this lifetime is done, we will return from whence we came, into the bosom of the universe, where we will decide our next life and review the last one.
It took me almost 35 years to get from hope to belief to knowing and sometimes I still fall back. I still question the universe for I too am still learning and will be for the rest of my life.

For me the journey began as a teenager, I just was not comfortable with the answers I had been given up until then about religion, God and the like. Most of it was too contradictory or just did not make sense to me. How could God be on the one hand jealous and vengeful and loving and caring on the other? Those qualities seemed more human than god like! Was he not God?

Even though I was told that God was all seeing, all knowing, all-powerful, in other words omnipotent, he acted an awful lot like humans. Yet we were supposed to be made in His likeness, which if He truly acted like us, I guess we have been. It also seemed that He spent a great deal of time wanting to punish us for violating quite arbitrary rules and laws. As I understood it, just about anything could be interpreted as a sin. You could almost not help but be a sinner and yet I was told that I had free will. Some people even told me that I was born a sinner! They informed me that God was really a god of fear and retribution and I really did not want any part of that. Yet I was supposed to worship God. Why would I worship someone or something that was so mean, someone who it seemed I could not please no matter how hard I tried?

My poor Mom, I asked her some really tough questions and she tried her best to give me the answers but at times even she seemed equally confused by it all. It was in church youth group with Reverend Gephart that I finally got to ask all the questions I desperately needed the answers to and to someone who should know, I mean after all he was a man of the cloth. Surely, he would have the answers.

Sometimes I think I caused Rev. Gephart more grief than was necessary but I just really needed to know. Much to my surprise, I was told that the answers to my questions would not be found in any book or in any building. The answers, he told me, were inside of me and that I would do just as well talking directly to

God and seeing what I felt about the answers I received.

I tried what Rev. Gephart suggested and the answers came. Sometimes it took me awhile to grasp the concepts and some I still do not quite understand to this day. I often still asked questions of both Rev. Gephart and Father Kish and they would do their best to give me an answer. But most of it I found inside of me.

So, I continued to study various religious writings and continued to ask questions and finally I came to that place of knowing. The more I studied the different religions the more I came to realize that they were based upon the same principles and the more I realized that religion was a man-made concept.
All along, prophets like Jesus, Buddha and Mohammad were trying to simply tell us that we and God are one and the same. We have the power within us (free will) to decide how our lives are going to go. God does not want to punish us for in fact God would be punishing God. Once I discovered who I really was, I looked at the world and all of its inhabitants in a much different light.

Now, getting to the point of knowing has not meant that my life has been perfect. In the overall scheme of things it has been perfect since I am creating it all, but I still have my ups and downs and for some reason the universe still tosses me a curve ball once in a while. Since I am so much more at peace with it all now; one day I will knock that curve ball out of the park. For now, I continue my journey knowing that at any moment I can choose something new for myself!

I know that I know what I know. It is not enough to believe it, you must know it. It is not enough to know it, you must show it. It is not enough to show it, you must live it!

But, how do you know that you know? It is very simple, I just know and so will all of us. We will know when we can make conscious decisions about our lives without fear, guilt and anxiety, for we will KNOW that the outcome will be exactly what we asked for. We will know when we can face life with peace and serenity and go with the flow instead of fighting the current. We will know when we realize that we are all interconnected; humans, nature, the seen and the unseen. We will know when we can face each day with the wonder of possibilities. And we will know that we can take a very different path to knowing and we will all reach the same destination, to a place of oneness!

JOURNAL AREA:

_____

_____

_____

_____

_____

_____

_____

_____

_____

_____

_____

_____

_____

_____

_____

JOURNAL AREA:

_____

_____

_____

_____

_____

_____

_____

_____

_____

_____

_____

_____

_____

_____

_____

Chapter 2: **Give & Receive**

"God has given us two hands, one to receive with and the other to give with." - Billy Graham

Give

Giving is a principle of Rare Sense because it is in the giving that we truly receive. I am not talking about giving for the mere sake of giving, but giving from the heart and soul. It is like Mother Theresa once said, "It is not the giving but the love you put in the giving, it is not the doing but the love you put in the doing."

When we give we are telling the universe we care not only about others but our own well being because the acts of giving show love and compassion. The interesting thing about giving is that in most cases we actually end up receiving more than we gave.

I know people who have spent time helping out Habitat for Humanity, a non-profit organization that builds houses for the less fortunate of us. They have told me that not only did it make them feel good to a part of such a worthwhile project, but they actually learned about drywall or roofing, information they can use later on their own home.

When I spend time coaching youth basketball, I get more out of seeing the young girls learn the game of basketball, build their own confidence and self-esteem than any win could provide. The mere sight of them scoring a basket or making a great pass warms me inside like almost nothing else. I do not coach youth sports for my own edification, and I certainly come away from it feeling all warm and toasty inside because I am giving of myself to the betterment of others.

"If you always give, you will always have."

- Chinese Proverb

Giving is also part of the natural laws of the universe, which is why it has been said that whatever we give we will receive back tenfold. Now, some people think that if we give $10 to some charity we will get $100 back somewhere else; however, that may or may not be the actual case. What I believe is being said here is that what we give we will get back and in greater quantity than you gave in the first place. It may be in more money but it just may be an increased feeling of happiness because we were caring and compassionate.

Whatever we do, we should not give through guilt and do not feel guilty if we cannot give at one time or another. It does no good to give out of guilt for either us or the person or organization we are giving to. Doing things through guilt only increases stress, anxiety and guilt. We should not give beyond our means but give freely of what we have to give. One thing everyone can give in abundance is love!

Some people think that giving means money and that is not necessarily the case. Actually giving your time to something can be more valuable than money. In the society we live in today that may not necessarily be the case but let's really examine this concept. We are a commodity driven society, with an economic system based on supply and demand and yet most of us think that money is more valuable than time. However, time is the one asset that we have very little, if no, control over. We have no idea how long we have in this lifetime and we know that once time is gone, there is no way we can get it back.

However, we can always get money and there is no limit to how much money we can get. Because of circumstances and the way they think some would disagree with what I just said but I know people who have sold their plasma to get money. I know people who have worked three jobs, played music, washed cars, mowed lawns or sold things on E-bay to get money. The ability for someone to make money is only limited by their imagination and creativity.

We have complete control over that. So, it is quite obvious that time and not money is more precious and valuable. So, if you can give your time to something, you have given much more than money could ever buy!

In this regard, whatever you have to give, make sure you give from the heart. Do not expect anything in return and you will receive more than you ever dreamed possible.

"It is expressly at those times when we feel needy that we will benefit the most from giving."

- Ruth Ross

Receive

Why are we generally so good at giving and so bad at receiving? Why do we feel guilty when we get something? How many of us find it hard to tell people what we want when they ask, as in birthdays or Christmas? Being able to receive things is also a principle of rare sense because the universe will give us everything we ask for, everything we desire, everything we dream of.

From my observation, we actually seem to enjoy making ourselves feel guilty when we receive something. Sometimes we feel that we have to give something back just because we received something. So, we immediately return a compliment or run out and buy something for the person who just gave us something, or we buy them lunch or anything, just to relieve the guilt and return the favor. That, however, is not necessary. We should not feel guilt, but joy. We need to rejoice in both the giving and receiving because both are gifts from the universe.

Some of us have even been programmed to immediately wonder what the ulterior motive of the giver is; what do they want in return, as if the mere act of giving something could not have been their one and only motive. Just like me, I am sure all of us have run into people who in fact did have an ulterior motive but we need not look for it. Instead let us look for the good always and the bad will simply no longer exist.

We even have trouble receiving a compliment. I know so many people who will actually either deny the compliment or feel that they have to put themselves down after receiving a compliment to kind of even the slate. Something like this.
"Boy, Ann, you really look beautiful tonight!"

"What?" "My hair is a mess, my make-up is wearing off and

just look at this chipped nail polish!"

How about this one?

"Tom, nice job with the presentation. You really knocked them dead in there today!"

"Are you kidding?" "I stumbled all over myself." "That had to be the worst job I have ever done!"

Or perhaps this one?
"George, Thanks for helping out with the party. We could not have done it without you!"

"I am not the one you should be thanking, I didn't do much."

Instead of all that, why not just say "Thanks, I appreciate it!"

Of course, we do not want to get a big head or anything. God help us if we actually believed the good things that people are saying about us. That would be vain and we need to be humble! I am telling you right now it is neither vain nor a lack of humility for you to accept anything, even a compliment from another.

How many times have you heard this comment after someone gives a compliment to someone else?

"Martha, you better stop or Bob is going to get a big head."

No, do not stop! Compliment each other! Tell each other how great, how wonderful, how beautiful they are. Be free with your gifts and compliments and be thankful in what you receive.

And when you receive a compliment or are given anything, accept it and receive it for the gift that it is, for to do less is to diminish the gift that you just received. And for God's sake, do not feel guilty when you receive something from another. Thank them and move on! I am quite certain that you will return the favor down the road. Accepting something that is given to you is the highest compliment you can return to the giver. It is also the way we show thanks to the universe for all that we have in our life.

It is funny because we are told it is better to give than to receive which makes us all feel guilty for receiving anything, but if there was no one to receive what we tried to give then how could we ever give anything? It really is just as nice to receive, as it is to give, we just have to stop feeling guilty about it! One way to help with the guilt, if you must feel guilt, is to honor the giver by paying it forward. If someone does or says something nice to you, then instead of doing something for that person (which remember diminishes the gift) then just do something or say something nice to someone else and pass on the gift!

The bottom line is that both giving and receiving are just as important, for without receivers there can be no givers and without givers there can be no receivers! In keeping with the laws of cause and effect, giving leads to receiving and vice versa! So both give and receive with a joyous heart for in both you are showing love!

JOURNAL AREA:

_____

_____

_____

_____

_____

_____

_____

_____

_____

_____

_____

_____

_____

Journal Area:

_____

_____

_____

_____

_____

_____

_____

_____

_____

_____

_____

_____

_____

_____

_____

_____

Chapter 3: **Create**

"Creativity comes from awakening and directing men's higher natures, which originate in the primal depths of the universe and are appointed by Heaven." - I-Ching

Here is something that is hard for a lot of people to accept. We are creating it all: the good, the bad, the ups, and the downs, all of it. We decided before we ventured to this earth plane exactly what basic type of life we would lead, who our parents would be, what experiences we would have, all of it! We are in control and have to accept responsibility for it. Because we have that control, otherwise known as free will, we can also change our path, destiny, whatever we want to call it by simply changing our minds.

It is so simple, it is complicated. It is simple, but I did not say it was easy. But that is what the universe is, simplicity and complexity at the same time. Sometimes it is so simple that we say it can not be the truth because the universe has to be much deeper and complicated.

We theorize, hypothesize and philosophize and come up with these complex systems to show how they all interact with one another just to conclude that it is in fact all related. All one! As quantum physicists, such as Deepak Chopra have said, "All made from the same stuff!" Look at how the inter-relational dependency comes full circle to the ultimate reality, we are creating and have created it all from the beginning of time and we will continue to do so! We are one with God or the universe because we are all a part of same whole. We are the universe and the universe is us. We are inseparable.

"The world we have created is a product of our thinking. It cannot be changed without changing our thinking."

- Albert Einstein

Let me demonstrate how we create our life. You see thoughts are in fact creative. Want an example? O.K. Look around you and check out all the things you see. Were those things not once just a thought in someone's mind? And from that thought did these things not take material form? Did we always have computers, toasters, microwaves and polyester clothes? Did the dwelling you reside in always exist? How did the pyramids come into form? How about sailing ships and flying machines? Everything man-made was once a thought, an idea, a dream, if you will!

If you believe that God created the heavens and earth, even that had to begin as a thought in God's mind!

"The only job we have been given when we came to this earth is to create. Everything we do is a creation, from a job, to children to thoughts. We all create all the time, it is all we do."

- Tom Justin

We are creating our reality everyday. When we wake up in the morning by our mere thoughts we can create whatever day we want. If we decide to be grouchy and mean spirited we will create a rotten day. Think happy and healthy and have a wonderful day.

OK, so what if you are thinking happy and the day is going well, but your boss yells at you and ruins the day. What about that? The answer? We choose how we are going to react to what happened and if we allow it to ruin our good day then that is totally up to us. We can not blame it on our boss because we still create the reaction to the negative stimulus.

You see, our thoughts are so powerful they can shift our mood in an instant. We can go from happy to sad quicker than the speed of light, more like at the speed of thought.

And lest we think differently, this is us doing it. The universe gave us the ability and the free will to use our thoughts in any way we see fit. We have complete control over our thoughts and the actions they produce.

Oh great, so I guess what you are saying is that I have no one to blame but myself. No, what I am saying is first get rid of blame for blame is negative and unnecessary, where as responsibility is positive. Take responsibility then understand that if we do not like the way that something is going, we can simply change it by changing our thoughts about it.

"If you don't like how things are, change it! You're

not a tree. You have the ability to totally transform every area in your life - and it all begins with your very own power of choice."

- Jim Rohn

Do you not understand what a powerful thing this is? Our thoughts are creative, so use them to create the world and life that we truly deserve and if this is what we feel we truly deserve, then it is not for me or anyone else to say that we chose wrong. It is up to us to decide but if things are not going the way we feel they should be then do something about it or maybe do nothing, it is after all our choice!

OK, so my thoughts are creative and I am responsible for them. If that is so, then why are you telling me that I am doing it wrong? That the world is not the way it should be?

I did not tell you that, I said that if we do not like the way it is going then change it and I am giving suggestions how we might change it to fit what we want to experience as a spiritual being. If we want the world and people to be more spiritual, then we need to think more spiritually. If we choose to do that, then that is the life and world that we will create for ourselves.

However, if life is not going the way we want it to and we ask for guidance from someone else and they tell us the truth, do not think they are being judgmental. They are simply pointing out what we asked them to tell us. Sometimes we even attack those very people from whom we seek help, mainly because we do not want to face the truth and take responsibility. It is so much easier to blame others when things go wrong!

> **"You are today where your thoughts have brought you; you will be tomorrow where your thoughts take you."**
>
> *- James Allen*

Like God said in "Conversations With God", if you tell me you want to go to San Francisco and you are heading to San Jose and I tell you so, am I judging you or simply pointing out that you are going the wrong way, given where you told me you want to go?

One area that I get into later involves creative thought and the media. I am telling you right here and now that the world is in the mess that it is in because what we focus on the bad, not the good, the negative not the positive, and the media is the main culprit here.

There are millions of good things that happen everyday, yet all the media seems to want to focus on is the bad. The good things outweigh the bad a million to one but they concentrate on the bad and then try to blame us for it by saying that is what people want to hear about. Are they sure? Have you ever seen a newscast or news show where they concentrated on the positive things that happen day to day? When they advertise their show do they highlight the good or bad stories? In most cases, probably 95% of the time, they highlight the bad.

Why do drug dogs in the school make the front page but the choir winning an award gets buried in the middle somewhere?

Why does the vandalism of school busses hit the news but the national honor society induction does not?

For every decade since I can remember, which started in the 60's, why has the media claimed that the youth of America is bad? They have been wrong every time and yet it perpetuates itself? You would think that those who grew up listening to this crap being said about them would want to change what they focus on. It is time for a major paradigm shift in the media. Let's start focusing on the good, the positive, the wonderful things that happen in daily life and we will create a world to reflect our thoughts. But if we continue to focus and think about the negative, that is exactly what we will continue to get. It is a simple thing and everyone says they want a better world, then why don't we do it?

"To decide to be at the level of choice is to take responsibility for your life and to be in control of your life."

- Arbie M. Dale

Beyond just our thoughts we actually have the ability to create life and there is no more powerful a creation than that. Yet again we think we are limited creatures with limited abilities. Often we are taught that so others can have control over us. But we are not limited; we are limitless for as long as we have the ability to think and create we are just as powerful as anything in the universe.

Remember, our thoughts are creative, so if we think about and focus on the negative, that is what we will create, a negative world, a negative society and a negative life. It is high time we all started to focus on the beauty of nature and mankind. For it is in each and every mind where we are creating our daily existence. If we want a world of love, peace, harmony and compassion, we must think love, peace, harmony and compassion. If we would all simply do that then we would get a world of love, peace, harmony and compassion.

"Be the change you seek in the world!"

- Mahatma Ghandi

JOURNAL AREA:

_____

_____

_____

_____

_____

_____

_____

_____

_____

_____

_____

_____

_____

_____

Chapter 4: **Responsibility**

"Enlightenment means
taking full responsibility
for your life." - William Blake

One of the biggest challenges in this modern age seems to be taking responsibility for our actions. We try to blame others for our very existence and our life and quickly look to lay responsibility elsewhere than at our own doorstep.

But this is really not possible since we are creating it all. However, if you believe that you do not have control, that you do not create your existence, then it is much easier to not take responsibility for it and to blame others.

As a child, we may lack the maturity as to how to respond to negative things said about us and thus are limited in our ability to choose what to believe. It is especially more difficult when the people who are supposed to love and protect us are the very ones causing the pain. However, once we mature and can make those informed, intelligent choices we can no longer blame others for the choices we make. Of course even children have the wisdom to choose to accept what is said about them. We can choose to internalize it or let it roll of our backs, like water off a duck. Very early on, we sometimes have a better understanding of who we really are. It is when we get older and start accepting someone else's version of who we are that we start to doubt ourselves.

One of the best examples of not taking responsibility for our actions involved the lawsuit against McDonald's by the lady who placed the coffee cup between her legs and burned herself. Had rare sense been applied in this situation, that lawsuit would have been thrown out, but in this day and age we are quicker to blame others than ourselves. Let me ask this question? Did any McDonald's employee place that cup between that lady's legs or did she choose to do that herself? I know you know the answer, so why was she not made to take responsibility for her own actions?

"I believe that we are solely responsible for our choices, and we have to accept the consequences of every deed, word, and thought throughout our lifetime."

- Elisabeth Kubler-Ross

Taking responsibility for our lives is the rare sense or spiritual thing to do. I have said earlier, we always take responsibility when things are going well, but we want to blame others when it is not. Convenient isn't it?

Well, that is simply not the way things work in the universe. We were given free will. We are responsible for our lives and the decisions we make. Yes, there are some things that happen to us that make us think that sometimes we are not in control. However, if we really look at our lives, the things that have happened and what our responses to those things have been, we will find that somehow, some way, we created it.

Looking in that mirror is one of hardest things we will ever do, but we must. Because until we do, we will not be able to change our circumstances for we will think that we do not have control, yet what we think about is brought to us.

So, if you think you are not responsible and that you do not have control, things will continue to be created in which you do not have control and your life will seem like it is one disaster after another. Taking responsibility is taking control and having control is using your free will.

Here is something that is going to sound contradictory, so please bear with me. We can think we are not responsible but we still are. We can think we are not in control but we still are. We can think that we do not have free will but we still do. For you see, we have free will and that is one thing that does not change about us. With that free will we are free to think whatever we want to think, but no matter what we think we are responsible for all of it. Either what happens to us or how we are going to react to it. And with that comes responsibility.

If things are not going the way we wish them to be, then we need to take the time to see what thoughts and decisions we have made to create the circumstances we face today. Sometimes we have to go back many years to find the answer, sometimes just a few seconds but we will find the answer because it lies within us.

The good and bad, the ups and downs, all of it! Being responsible is having rare sense because we are telling the universe; I understand who I am and what I am capable of. I understand that I have the gift of free will and that I use that gift each and every moment of every single day! I am in control and I am a creative being, one with God and an integral part of the universe.

"Let us not talk of karma, but simply of responsibility toward the whole world."

- His Holiness the Dalai Lama

JOURNAL AREA:

_____

_____

_____

_____

_____

_____

_____

_____

_____

_____

_____

_____

_____

_____

JOURNAL AREA:

_____

_____

_____

_____

_____

_____

_____

_____

_____

_____

_____

_____

_____

_____

Chapter 5: **Live**

"Life is what we make it,
always has been, always
will be." - Grandma Moses

If we are to have rare sense we must truly be alive. You have heard the expression before of "being in the moment". "Be here now" is another way of saying it. How about, "live your life to the fullest". All of these are comments on the art of living and living is using your rare sense indeed.

It involves all of our senses; touch, smell, hearing, sight, taste and psychic abilities. It involves all three parts of our being; body, mind and spirit. It involves balance and synchronicity. It involves acknowledging who we are, a spiritual being in human form.

Living means to take risks, for the greater the risk the greater the reward. Living means to love with all of your being. It means being passionate about our life work. It means finding your purpose and pursuing it with determination. Living means finding the possible in the impossible, to dream, to aspire, to hope, to believe and to know.

Living means we must nurture all three parts of our being. We must exercise the mind, the body and the spirit. This can be done in so many ways they are too numerous to mention, but here are some examples: read up on something new, physical exercise, good nutrition and meditation.

We are living when we try and experience all that life has to offer us. When we try new foods, study different cultures and religions, spend time with friends and family, do volunteer work, exercise, travel to new places, play and meet new people, we are truly living.

By living we are trying to experience all we can so that this time on this planet can be used to its fullest and we can reach our fullest potential. In life, we know there will be good times and bad, births and deaths, marriages and divorces and that we can learn something from all that life has to offer.

As a spiritual being, sometimes living in this human form can be frustrating and confining if we allow it to be. But we know that our time here will be brief and that one day we will return to the universe and all the knowledge contained therein.

People with rare sense live life with gusto. We see each moment as another chance to create life anew and as another opportunity to experience the wonder of it all. Some of us even choose to do so with reckless abandon, which from time to time may be a good idea, though I would not necessarily recommend it on a daily basis.

Rare Sense tells us that in this life there are only those limits we place on it and there is an abundance of everything. There is no reward without risk. That peace and harmony are a mere thought away. That to soar like an eagle you have to let your feet leave the ground. That to be child-like is a natural way to be. That change is constant, it is inevitable, it is life.

This life is a journey and like any journey, this lifetime will one day come to an end. How are we living our lives? Are we cherishing each and every moment or do we struggle through our days? Are we living in the moment and do we see the joy and simplicity of it all, or do we see nothing but pain and sorrow? How our lives go is up to us but know that there is a wonderful, beautiful world out there for us to enjoy, we simply have to choose to do so!

JOURNAL AREA:

_____

_____

_____

_____

_____

_____

_____

_____

_____

_____

_____

_____

_____

_____

_____

Chapter 6: **Permit**

"We need to give ourselves permission to act out our dreams and visions, not look for more sensations, more phenomena, but live our strongest dreams -- even if it takes a lifetime." - Vijali Hamilton

Let the universe flow through you. Permit yourself to express your emotions and permit others to do the same. We must permit ourselves to be happy, sexual, funny, tired, crazy, sad, powerful, successful, intimate, loving, caring, compassionate, passionate, hopeful, energetic, healthy, determined, creative, angry, envious, beautiful, to have dreams, to have goals, to have a life. Then permit others to do the same.

The reason I said permit yourself and others to do these things is that we tend to wrap guilt into them. And if we are not making ourselves feel guilty over it, then others will gladly try to do it to us. Guilt is the ego's way of continuing the illusion and not permitting us to see who we really are because the ego does not want to give up the control it has over us. Other people use guilt to try and control us also. Most major religions use guilt to try and get people to obey the rules. Without guilt, people would actually realize that we are in control of our lives and that just does not suit some people or groups because it is usually those people or institutions that think they will lose power. It is that ego thing again!

But power over what or whom? Those people who try and use guilt and control to remain in power, actually find out that those they are controlling will eventually rebel against it. Simply because it is not the natural order of things and the more people grow spiritually, the more they realize that they actually have had the control all along. We begin to question everything including those that have controlled us through such things as guilt. Then the one thing that was feared is realized. They do lose power and they created the situation to cause that to happen.

The funny thing is if you permit people to discover who they really are and to live their life free from judgment and guilt, we will actually find that there is no loss of power but a sharing of it. When we permit another to live their life we are actually making both them and us more powerful because we are both tapping into the immense power of the universe.

Permitting others to better themselves allows you to better yourself. Permitting is an act of unconditional love. It allows each of us to become all that we are capable of being. When we permit others to be all they can be, we automatically do the same for ourselves and what a wonderful thing that is!

So permit yourself and everyone else to live, to express themselves and to better themselves. For in permitting people to live you can eliminate evil, which is merely "live" spelled backwards. Things that we call "evil" are simply things that are not living, for if you truly permit yourself and others to live, you will no longer have "evil"!

JOURNAL AREA:

_____

_____

_____

_____

_____

_____

_____

_____

_____

_____

_____

_____

_____

_____

JOURNAL AREA:

_____

_____

_____

_____

_____

_____

_____

_____

_____

_____

_____

_____

_____

_____

_____

Chapter 7: **Serve**

"Only a life lived in the service to others is worth living." - Albert Einstein

Service to yourself and others is another principle of Rare Sense. It is in this service that we learn about ourselves and others, and in doing so we come more into realization that we are all in this together.

Serving others is our way of giving back all that we have received. It is our way of honoring the innate spirituality in ourselves and others. It is how we care for one another and show love and compassion. It is what brings us together when there are so many things we use to pull us apart.

Being of service makes your heart smile and your soul sing. It is how we show that we care for one another. It is how we express the spiritual side of ourselves. It is how we get in touch with our spiritual side and demonstrate our rare sense. And being of service to ourselves is just as important as being of service to others because by helping ourselves, we automatically help others. When we grow, we all grow for we are all one.

As Wayne Dyer has said, "We are all a part of the Universe, uni meaning one, verse meaning song. Universe = one song" A song we all sing when we are letting our soul guide us in being of service. And this is not just service to humans but to all creatures, all of nature and all of life. We must care for everyone and everything as if our life depends on it, for in fact it does.

"Every day use your magic to be of service to others."

Marcia Wieder

Nothing is truly separate in the universe. All the artificial walls we build to separate ourselves are just an illusion. Our soul craves service because when we are in service we are showing love, one of the constants in the universe. In that moment of service we are in direct contact with our soul and the universe. We are again one!

And it is in this service to others and everything that we can truly see and experience the innate goodness of man, when we can feel and experience the love emanating from everything. When the universe and all that is in it is in harmony!

The next time you are serving yourself or another, take a moment to stop and pay attention to how you feel and you will see what I mean. It is a joyous, loving moment, one that you will want to duplicate again and again. I have often said that I get more out of serving that I actually think I give. I feel that way because I know that it is in this state of service that I am being as spiritual as I can possibly be!

JOURNAL AREA:

_____

_____

_____

_____

_____

_____

_____

_____

_____

_____

_____

_____

_____

_____

JOURNAL AREA:

_____

_____

_____

_____

_____

_____

_____

_____

_____

_____

_____

_____

_____

_____

Chapter 8: **Love & Compassion**

"Love alone can unite living beings so as to complete and fulfill them... for it alone joins them by what is deepest in themselves. All we need is to imagine our ability to love developing until it embraces the totality of men and the earth." - Albert Einstein

Love

There is something I want to say to begin this chapter that you have probably heard before but it bears repeating here. Love is all there truly is, everything else is an illusion that we create. We are pure love, pure light, pure energy.

Before you can truly love another you must first love yourself. Showing love to yourself is not a selfish act, it is a necessary one because you are part and parcel of the universe just like everything else, so by loving yourself, you love God, for you are God. I believe it was stated something like this: man was made in the image and likeness of God.

We are pure energy and pure love. Like change, love is a constant in the universe, in fact there is only love. Everything else is an illusion designed to allow us to experience other things. We were born from love and we shall return to love. There is no judgment day, no eternal damnation; those are human constructs, not spiritual ones.

God is not so petty as to withhold love and to punish us for disobeying his commands. Would you really want a God like that? It does not sound godlike, it sounds more human like which is actually what that is. Man in trying to explain the universe has also tried to put a human face on God with all the human misgivings and shortcomings. But if that were in fact the case, then God would not be a god at all.

No, love is what God is, always has been and always will be. Every action of a human being comes from two different emotions: love or fear, and fear is nothing more than, as Wayne Dyer said, "False Evidence Appearing Real." Love truly does conquer all.

Those that have had near death experiences have all reported practically the same experience. They were overwhelmed by the absolute powerful feeling of love. It came from everywhere and simply filled them up. A love like they had never experienced on earth because it was a spiritual love, directly from God. In spirit form we are love, for there is nothing else to be.

Unconditional love like that is hard to accomplish on this earth plane because we are here to experience all that life has to offer, which means all the emotions and their opposites. The question is, are we able to make this earth plane one where unconditional love is the constant, as in the spirit world? I believe it is possible and will one day happen. It will happen when we all discover who we really are.

When will this happen? That is hard to say. We are still at a very primitive state with us looking more at our differences and, in fact, finding differences to keep us apart. Teacher after teacher, prophet after prophet have tried to show us the way to being one again and we have not come very far. I know it will happen one day, I just do not know when. This I can say, the teachers will keep coming and keep teaching until we finally get it and when we do, all of heaven and earth will rejoice.

Love is a glorious thing! When it is shared unconditionally it is the most wonderful thing one can ever experience. The closest I have come to it thus far has been with my mother, brother, wife and a few friends and that has been wonderful enough. Now I try and approach every situation from a position of love and I have found that things go a lot smoother and the experience is much better.

I am still working on loving everyone unconditionally. I do this because I want to experience that sense of oneness with all, like I experience with a few! When I am with those that I love unconditionally it is the safest, most wonderful place to be. Sometimes it is like time stands still or in fact the illusion of time is gone for there is only bliss.

Now that I have experienced this on the earth plane from time to time, when I allow it to happen and try not to judge it, I want it all the time. So I know it is possible to change this world and make it a place of peace, harmony and total love. I believe that if you can experience it anytime, you can experience it all the time.

Let's make love our constant companion and watch the world change day by day. If we can simply approach things from a position of love, we will in fact have heaven on earth.

Compassion

"Compassion is the antitoxin of the soul: where there is compassion even the most poisonous impulses remain relatively harmless."

- Eric Hoffer

As people with rare sense, we know that having compassion for ourselves and all other beings in our universe means we have a true understanding that we are spiritual beings in human form. We know deep down in our souls that the plight of others is also our plight. Compassion shows us without a shadow of a doubt that we are all connected, we are all one. Compassion is another side of love!

And since we are all one, showing compassion for others is also showing compassion for ourselves.

Compassion is what gets us to volunteer at the soup kitchen, for Meals on Wheels, or at the local shelter. It is what gets us to donate to charities and speak out against injustice. Being compassionate allows our spirit to soar and soul to sing.

"I feel the capacity to care is the thing which gives life its deepest significance."

- Pablo Casals

When we are being compassionate we cannot help but feel wonderful, for we are helping others and anytime we help others it just feels good. In fact, showing compassion is another way of expressing love.

Compassion assists us in understanding each other because it opens communication. When someone else sees that you are being compassionate towards them, they feel the love radiating from you and it helps them to want to connect.

People with rare sense are compassionate people, which makes us excellent listeners and listening is the most important part of communication. And we do not just listen with our ears but with our entire body. Compassionate people listen with our very souls.

Some people say that compassion is a human weakness instead of a strength. I do not know about you but I actually feel sorry for people who feel this way because they are disconnected from the universe and that has to be painful.

I remember a story that most of you probably have heard since it has been passed around through e-mails for some time. It is the story about the little boy who is walking down the beach tossing star fish back into the water. A man sees him and approaches the little boy. The man tells him that it was a waste of time and it could not possibly matter since there were so many star fish and he was the only person helping them and he could not possibly help them all. But the little boy simply picked up another starfish, tossed it back into the ocean and stated, "It mattered to that one!" That my friends, is being compassionate!

It did not matter that he could not help all of them; he simply wanted to help and do what we could. If we all showed the same compassion as that little boy I dare to say we would change the world and probably save a lot more starfish!

Showing compassion is not just for us human beings. We need to show compassion for all living things for we are connected to them too. One is not exclusive of the other!

"Until he extends his circle of compassion to include all living things, man will not himself find peace."

- Albert Schweitzer

JOURNAL AREA:

_____

_____

_____

_____

_____

_____

_____

_____

_____

_____

_____

_____

_____

JOURNAL AREA:

_____

_____

_____

_____

_____

_____

_____

_____

_____

_____

_____

_____

_____

_____

_____

Chapter 9: **Forgive**

"To forgive is the highest, most beautiful form of love. In return, you will receive untold peace and happiness." - Robert Muller

Forgiveness, what a beautiful thing! It is the ultimate expression of love for in forgiveness we tell ourselves and the world that we have compassion.

Forgiving oneself and others takes a great burden off our shoulders. All the anger, hurt, resentment and guilt that was weighing us down simply vanishes when we choose to forgive.

Like other things that I have written about in this book, we want to start by forgiving ourselves for the perceived transgressions we have committed both against ourselves and others. These acts carry such a heavy burden that they can affect all aspects of our lives, from our health to our mental state to our spiritual state.

By forgiving ourselves we can cleanse our soul and start anew. We understand that we are in human form and not perfect. We are going to make choices that do not work for us and when we recognize that we have made a choice that does not work, through forgiveness we can say, "That's OK, let me choose differently." Through forgiveness, we tell ourselves that we are still a loving, caring, and compassionate human being capable of making mistakes but also just as capable to correct them. It forces us to take responsibility for our own choices but also to see that we do have the ability to create everything anew with different choices. Forgiveness puts the power and control squarely back onto us.

When we forgive ourselves, we are truly loving ourselves and acknowledging our spirit. Once we can forgive ourselves then we can take the next step and forgive others. As it says in the Lords Prayer, "forgive us our trespasses, as we forgive those who trespass against us."

As I stated earlier, forgiving others for their transgressions allows us to take back both the control and power in our lives. As long as we hold a grudge or resentment of others for what they did to us, we continue to give power to both that person and that event to have some control over our lives. The more we dwell on the transgression, the more we conjure up the old emotional injury, which in turn continues to give it life. This can suck the very power out of us and places it back to the person who caused the transgression.

To break this vicious and quite damaging cycle, all we have to do is forgive that person and move on. This does not mean that the event did not occur, but this simple act drains it of all its power to continue to injure us. Without the power to control or do damage we can begin the healing process and move on.

Is it easy? Yes and no. Depending on the degree of emotional attachment we have to the situation, it may take a while to truly forgive but if we focus on love, compassion and goodness, we will find it easier and easier to do.

It took me a while to forgive my father for what I perceived were transgressions on his part by not being a "good" father to me. We did not talk for several years and I harbored a deep seeded anger over his incapacity to express love. I really thought that he neither loved me nor was proud of me.

Unfortunately, it was not until he passed from this earth plane that

I learned the truth. Once I did, I found the strength to forgive him and in turn learned a lot about myself and him. It was one of the most profound moments in my life and helped me to be better at forgiveness.

It made it much easier to forgive my first wife for her perceived transgressions in our marriage, as well as to forgive myself for the choices I made, like choosing to marry her in the first place. It allowed me to take the control and power back. Forgiveness forces me to take responsibility for my actions. It allows me to release the anger and hurt. It allows me to see her as another human being with all the frailties of all human beings and view her with more compassion then I ever thought possible.

Forgiveness will lighten the load and free your soul. It shows both compassion for yourself and others. So the next time you think you screwed up or somebody hurt you in some way, do not judge but simply forgive, forgive, and forgive some more and then you can move on.

JOURNAL AREA:

_____

_____

_____

_____

_____

_____

_____

_____

_____

_____

_____

_____

_____

_____

_____

Chapter 10: **Learn & Teach**

"There is only one thing more painful than learning from experience and that is not learning from experience." - Archibald McLeish

Learn

People with rare sense are in a constant state of learning. We are learning about ourselves and we are learning about others.

All along the way in our life we are learning, for life is the greatest school of all. Another word for it is experiencing. Every day of our lives our soul is learning. We come here to experience and learn.

Some of the greatest times I have spent have been experiencing things I have never experienced before. From reading different religious texts to simply talking with people of other races or cultures. From eating food I have never before eaten to observing nature in all its wonder. Learning helps us to grow as a person. Learning helps us be more compassionate and understanding.

Ignorance on the other hand, which is nothing more than a lack of knowledge, can lead us into all kinds of trouble. I know that a lot of the challenges we face in the world today with our fellow human beings is simply our own ignorance. If we simply took the time to learn more about one another, I know we would have less conflict in the world. We would communicate better and be able to find more common ground then we think now exists. So to grow spiritually, we must learn and experience all we can for the more knowledgeable we become about ourselves and the world we live in the more we can help to bring about positive changes for everyone.

Take the time to learn and/or experience something new every day, whether it be about yourself or the world in which we all live. This is how you live life to the fullest!

Teach

"A teacher affects eternity; he can never tell where his influence stops."

- Henry Brooks Adams

People with rare sense are not only learning but are also teaching. By our own actions we are showing the world that there is a better way replete with love, compassion and harmony. Sure if you pick up the newspaper and watch the news it will seem that we are not making progress at all. We however understand that what is portrayed in the media is a very small percentage of what is actually happening on a daily basis. So, we continue to show the world, sometimes one person at a time, what we have learned and what we know.

The really wonderful thing about teaching others is that we cannot help but to also learn from what we are trying to teach, for in our teachings are also lessons and so the teacher becomes the student. We also know that we do not know everything, that we still have much to learn and so even though we are teaching we simply are also learning. There again is the wonderful balance of the universe.

Some of us teach openly by actively conducting seminars and speaking to people about spirituality. There are those that do it from the pulpit and those that teach about compassion and kindness through literature, song and art.

Have you not noticed the proliferation of books, television shows, movies and songs that over the past several years have opened our eyes to all things spiritual?

Even the medical establishment is slowly acknowledging alternative procedures and teaching them in our medical schools. Eastern and Western medicine is slowly merging into a cohesive system and changing the very foundation of medicine.

Most of us simply teach others about love, compassion and harmony through the actions of our daily lives by doing random acts of kindness, volunteering to help others or simply passing on the ideals of love, compassion and harmony to our children.

Both methods are quite effective and will lead all of us to the same place, a world where love will rule the day. A world where compassion is king and harmony is queen. A world where there is a balance of the male and female energies. A world of peace and prosperity, where no one is persecuted simply because they are different. A world where everyone has the basic necessities of life and no one goes without shelter or food.

This is what we are teaching through our spiritual actions. We are creating a better world by simply showing the world a better way to live. Everyone is a teacher as well as a student. We equally share the responsibility of both roles and as long as we accept and acknowledge both roles we will continue to grow together and create a world in which we and our future generations will want to live.

JOURNAL AREA:

_____

_____

_____

_____

_____

_____

_____

_____

_____

_____

_____

_____

_____

JOURNAL AREA:

Chapter 11: **Trust**

"Have Faith in
God, but Trust your
"Cold Prickley's" - Gentle-Daydreamer

People with rare sense trust themselves; we trust our intuition and the universe. We know that everything happens for a reason and we trust the decisions and choices we have made in our lives because we know that those choices have created the experiences we have had and know those experiences were necessary for us in this lifetime.

We have a trust that comes from knowing who we are and what we know. A trust that is rooted deeply in our souls and that is unshakable and unending, in fact everyone is born with it. We trust in the wisdom and abundance of the universe for we know that it is also unending.

Those with a lack of trust in themselves and the universe have forgotten where we come from and who we are. We have allowed the opinions of others to influence how we see the world. We have learned to be distrustful but we can learn to trust again. It is our job to teach and show each other the way. We were born with a trustful nature. We trusted our parents would care for and love us. The only way we can become distrustful is to learn not to trust. But just as we can learn not to trust we can learn to trust again.

Trust in this day and age can be hard to regain for those without rare sense. As a society we have lost trust in our political leaders when it is evident that they do not have everyone's best interests at heart but merely their own. We have lost trust in a political system that does not include all political parties and all people but welcomes special interest money and the influence that comes with it.

We have lost trust in our corporate leaders as we continue to hear about yet another scandal at the highest levels of our corporate structure. We continue to see businesses exploiting workers everywhere but especially third world workers in an effort to simply increase profits. The bottom line is more important then the people, but what these so called leaders fail to see is that without the workers they would be nowhere. Trust is not a component of a corporate culture that through its very actions breeds distrust! How is it then that the companies that do support their workers and see their true value still are making a profit? The leaders of these companies have rare sense and year after year they are named the best companies in the world to work for.

We have lost trust in our religious leaders and institutions as sex scandals have rocked the very foundation of at least one major religion. Further, we have lost faith and trust in religious institutions that continue to preach about a God that is both vengeful and loving and continue to focus more on the rules than on the very people they are trying to lead. We have lost trust in leaders and institutions that continue to preach separateness and not togetherness. That continue to try and justify the killing of people based upon some religious writings and ignoring the basic fundamental teachings of all religions, that of love, compassion and charity!

Trust once lost is hard to get back, especially for those who are looking to the very institutions described above for guidance and getting nothing but contradiction.

Trust is hard to come by in a society where the media reports focus almost entirely on the "bad" things that happen and almost totally ignore the good, which actually is more of what happens over 90% of the time each day. Trust is lacking where sensationalism is more important than fact!

How do we learn to trust again? We need to start inside and start trusting our intuition, our gut feelings, our instincts, whatever you want to call it. It is the universe communicating with us and when we are distrustful we then ignore the very message coming from the universe. It must start there. We must have faith and know that we create the environment in which we live, so if we want to change that environment we must begin by changing ourselves. That begins when we trust ourselves, because by trusting ourselves we trust the universe.

Why do people with rare sense have trust when everything seems to go against it? It is because, as I stated earlier, we know what the truth is and we know that for us trust is as natural as breathing. It comes from our souls and no amount of negativity can get us to not trust both the universe and ourselves. We teach others to trust through our own actions knowing that it will lead to a more trusting society and that the universe will support us.

Without trust, a society will eventually become so distrustful that the very things we fear will come to be because we will have created the environment to make it so! Trust is at the very basis of love, so without trust we will not have love.

Fortunately, we know that trusting the universe and ourselves is where it all begins and from that will flow the love necessary to change this world!

"God has entrusted me with myself."

- Epictetus

JOURNAL AREA:

_____

_____

_____

_____

_____

_____

_____

_____

_____

_____

_____

_____

_____

_____

JOURNAL AREA:

Chapter 12: **Gratitude**

"Feeling grateful or appreciative of someone or something in your life actually attracts more of the things that you appreciate and value into your life." - Northrup Christiane

People with Rare Sense have gratitude and show gratitude in their daily lives. We know that there is always more to be thankful for then there is to complain about. If we truly take the time to reflect upon our life we will see this is true.

We need to spend some time writing down the things we are thankful for and thank everyone and everything on a daily basis for those things and we will see that our life has been wonderful and is full of promise rather than gloom and despair.

Having gratitude for our lives will open our eyes to all the possibilities still ahead. We will become more alive than we have ever been when we simply take time to be thankful.

Sure bad things have happened and may continue to happen in our lives but those times do not have to control our lives and predict our future. Recognizing and thanking the universe for all of it, the good and the bad, for all the events of our lives have shaped who we are today, allows us to openly acknowledge those events and to create our future without the burden of guilt, fear and anxiety for we know that we control our destiny through creative thought. We know that we experienced things for a reason and that we control our future.

Wallowing in self pity and blaming others only keeps us down. We cannot rise above those things if we stay stuck there. Showing gratitude frees us of those bonds and allows us to soar. It frees our souls and just like forgiveness, places the power right back into our hands.

When we say a prayer of gratitude, we are acknowledging to the universe that we are on a spiritual path and that everything and anything that has happened to us was of our own creation and that the future is full of possibilities and is under our control.

So, take the time everyday to say a prayer of gratitude. Every night take time to count the blessings of the day. Acknowledge what the universe has provided and give thanks, for this will truly help us on our spiritual journeys.

JOURNAL AREA:

_____

_____

_____

_____

_____

_____

_____

_____

_____

_____

_____

_____

_____

JOURNAL AREA:

_____

_____

_____

_____

_____

_____

_____

_____

_____

_____

_____

_____

_____

_____

Chapter 13: **Dream**

"I have a dream..."

- Dr. Martin Luther King

The dream for people with rare sense is the dream of all prophets, gurus and spiritual leaders. Just like Dr. King we have a dream of a better world, a world where we are all one in the spiritual sense, which will lead us all to being one in all the senses. Where everyone is treated equally and not judged by the color of their skin, their nationality, religion or anything else but simply on the fact that we are all a part of the same universe.

Some might say this dream is improbable at best to achieve, if not impossible. They do not have rare sense. Those of us with rare sense know that this dream is inevitable. We cannot tell exactly when this oneness will happen but we know that someday it will happen. What we are trying to accomplish in this lifetime is to move the world a little closer to the reality of all those prophets, seers, gurus and spiritual leaders, who came before us and are working with us today.

Impossible is not a word in our vocabulary because we know that nothing is impossible. Everything that we now have or see was once a dream of someone's that was brought into reality through thought based upon choice. Thoughts, ideas and dreams are all the same thing.

The forefathers of the United States had a dream of a country where everyone was equal, everyone mattered and no one should be judged. They had rare sense! We have not necessarily fulfilled that dream yet but like our overall dream for the entire world, we are working on it, which is the one reason why people flock to the United States. It is because we have this dream of a better life and that is very attractive to everyone.

Rare Sense people are dreamers. We dream of a better life, of a gentler more spiritual society that puts the emphasis on taking care of each other and the world in which we live. We dream of a society that some might call utopia and unattainable. They do not have rare sense. We dream because we know that the universe will give us whatever we ask for and dreaming is another way of asking for what we know is attainable, for the universe is abundance.

Now, some might say that we spend way too much time dreaming. Our answer to them is we spend time on things that we know are going to produce results. We also know that to be truly alive, you must dream. Those that do not dream are not fully participating in this lifetime for dreams are part of the creative process. And, where would we be without dreamers? Everything you see around you was at one time a dream, a thought, an idea. The type of dreams I am talking about are just another thought, another idea.

We are a different kind of dreamer. We are not your stereotypical day dreamer, even though we dream all the time. What makes us different is we dream with a purpose. We dream because we know that dreams are where it all begins, which is creation. Since our thoughts are creative so then are our dreams.

I am not necessarily talking about the dreams we have while we sleep even thought they too are part of the process. I am talking about our dreams that lead us to better ourselves and our society, dreams of world peace, dreams of ending hunger, eradicating disease, abolishing war.

People with rare sense are constantly working on this dream through their own thoughts, actions and deeds. Most of which you never hear about but then we are not looking for publicity or praise. We are simply doing what we inherently know to be right. We are following our universal dream and doing our best to teach and show others that we can realize our dream, if we simply live it everyday.

"Nothing is as real as a dream. The world can change around you, but your dream will not. Responsibilities need not erase it. Duties need not obscure it. Because the dream is within you, no one can take it away."

- Tom Clancy

Ours is the dream of oneness, wholeness, peace and harmony and though we are in human form, we are still spiritual beings. Our souls know all the secrets of the universe and we know that to make our dream a reality we simply must LIVE IT!

You may ask how I know that this dream can become our reality and I say to you, look around and observe. It is already coming about. The world is getting smaller, communication faster, knowledge freer. No longer can those trying to perpetrate disharmony, dysfunction and disinformation hide from the view of the world. The information is out, the disharmony revealed. Just 50 years ago, word about what was happening in Europe and Japan was slow in getting out. People intent on harming others had the advantage of time. They could perpetrate their acts and the world did not find out about it for quite awhile, if at all. Today, this happens very rarely for communication is lightening fast and available to more and more people.

The bad things happening behind the Iron Curtain were concealed behind that wall until the Internet came into being. Information replaced disinformation. The truth was revealed. Once truth is brought to light, it can never be contained again. Those of us with rare sense know that the dream will become reality because the truth is getting out and you cannot stop truth.

Even the terrorists of today know that they cannot stop the truth about their actions and their intent. This is why they have become more violent, for they are desperate. They know that eventually truth will win out and when that happens all their attempts at control and fear will be lost. Then they will lose the power they so desperately seek. Power that was never really power at all, for true power lies within the dream of oneness and love of one another. It never has nor never will lie in fear and intimidation.

Our dream is the promise of the universe. Our dream has oneness and love as its goal. Our dream seeks to help, seeks to encourage, seeks to support, seeks to build and seeks to embrace. This is the dream of oneness. This is the dream of people with rare sense and this dream we will make a reality.

JOURNAL AREA:

_____

_____

_____

_____

_____

_____

_____

_____

_____

_____

_____

_____

_____

JOURNAL AREA:

_____

_____

_____

_____

_____

_____

_____

_____

_____

_____

_____

_____

_____

_____

_____

_____

_____

Chapter 14: **Harmony**

"Harmony seldom makes
a headline." - Silas Bent

Harmony, balance and equality; different words with similar meanings. When speaking of these things I am not only talking about the harmony in nature but the harmony of our thoughts. When we are in harmony with nature and in balance with our thoughts and we treat everyone and everything equally, we are acting and thinking with rare sense. The universe has balance to it, where every action creates a reaction. Nature, when left alone and not disturbed is in harmony with itself. Everything that is needed is provided. When we treat one another equally, we are in balance with the universe and in harmony with nature.

Now, I am probably going to get the ire up with some of what I am about to say but that is what this is all about. I am trying to get you to think in a different, albeit "rare sense" way.

We give lip service to human rights. We give lip service concerning equality. We say the right things but do not back them up with action. We all want harmony, balance & equality as long as we do not lose anything ourselves. If having those things means giving up anything we currently have we find some reason why it will not be so good after all.

We have not found reasoning through rare sense but rather through earthly things. A truly spiritual person, one with rare sense, understands that for everyone to truly be equal, for us to have harmony and balance in this world, we all have to agree that no one person deserves more than another. Wow, wait a minute! Is that not Socialism or Communism you are talking about?

> **"Achieving a balanced life is a choice that each of us continually makes second by second, thought by thought, feeling by feeling. On the one hand, we can simply exist. But on the other, we can choose to pack out seconds and create valuable minutes in all aspects of our lives."**

- Mark Victor Hansen

Hardly! I am talking about harmony, balance and equality and if you notice what I actually said, it was that no one person deserves more than another. I did not say they could not have more than another. I said they do not deserve more than another. Now, if one person has more then another through their own efforts but at the same time does everything they can to make sure everyone has enough of what they need and in turn they still have more, than spiritually they know and are practicing rare sense and contributing to the harmony, balance and equality we say we are seeking.

> **"We hold these truths to be self-evident: that all men are created equal; that they are endowed by their Creator with certain unalienable rights; that among these are life, liberty, and the pursuit of happiness..."**

-Thomas Jefferson

As long as we understand that every human being deserves to be treated equally, then we will not think we are better than another.

We will treat everyone with respect, compassion and love. You see it is not harmony, balance and equality in physical things that I am talking about, it is in how we treat one another. Too many of us actually think we are better than others and deserve more than others and that is just not true!

You reap what you sow! If you want a society that values human rights, start treating everyone equally. If you want a world without war, start living in harmony with one another. If you want a world without hunger, create balance. Understand that no one deserves more and we will be on our way, as a society, to curing many, many woes.

Our egos tell us differently but ego is not spirit. If you simply listen to your soul, you will see that what I am saying is true. It even feels right. Why do we feel so good when we share and give back to others? Because our soul knows that when we share and treat each other equally, we are being as spiritual as possible. It makes our soul jump for joy.

One thing that is evident on this earth plane is that in physical things we will not be equal and no amount of government intervention will change that. It is not a political thing; it is the way of this earth. One person will have more stuff than another. One person may live in a bigger house and drive a bigger car. One person will be better looking; more physically fit, more successful or more intelligent than another. Some will live longer, some will live better, some will not live at all.

But if we treat each other equally and understand that all human beings deserve the basic necessities of life then we will have equality on this earth plane, which is the best we can ask for as spiritual beings in human form. We have limitations as humans but there is nothing that can not be overcome by spirit and that includes our own egos!

Some people talk about heaven on earth. We will get to heaven on earth if we use rare sense and treat everyone equally. We will get heaven on earth when we use our spiritually to truly have equality. It will not matter how much money we have, what religion we are, where we live or how we dress. The only thing that will matter is we see everyone as an equal and know that everyone deserves at least the basic necessities of life. No one will go hungry, no one will lack shelter and all will be free. Some having more but no one thinking they deserve more.

Harmony, balance and equality are three different words with similar meanings and three of the most powerful words in our language. If we can think and act with harmony, balance and equality, we are doing so with rare sense and will create the world we so badly say we want to live in.

> **"He who lives in harmony with himself lives in harmony with the universe."**
>
> *- Marcus Aurelius*

JOURNAL AREA:

_____

_____

_____

_____

_____

_____

_____

_____

_____

_____

_____

_____

_____

_____

JOURNAL AREA:

_____

_____

_____

_____

_____

_____

_____

_____

_____

_____

_____

_____

_____

_____

_____

Chapter 15:
Acceptance & Tolerance

"When you judge another, you do not define them, you define yourself." - Wayne Dyer

Acceptance

Why is it that we find it so difficult to accept ourselves the way we are and others the way they are? Why do we feel the need to try and change others to our view for them when we ourselves want to stay the same and resist changing to please others? Which by the way, we should not change to please others but rather to please us!

We know that we cannot change others, even though we are forever trying. They have to want to change themselves. We also know that we do not want to be judged but we still judge others. And we judge ourselves, usually much too harshly!

Why do we even find the need to judge at all? Fear, insecurity, and doubt, that's why! We do not feel good enough. We do not feel pretty enough. We do not feel smart enough. OK, why do we feel this way? Because we choose to feel this way.

Sure, in our past we may have been told we are not good enough, pretty enough or smart enough but that was the opinion of others and is not how it has to be today. We get programmed by all the propaganda laid onto us as we grow up and that helps shape our thinking when we become adults. However, once we become adults we have the choice to continue to think in this manner about ourselves or change the way we see, feel and think about ourselves. If we do not like our programming then we need to change it! Keep in mind this programming cannot necessarily be changed over night. We were not programmed over night, it happened over years. So, understand that it will take time and may not be easy, but it is simple.

People with rare sense understand that we control our thoughts, we create our world and so anything that happened to us or was said to us in the past only creates our future if we allow it to. If we think bad thoughts about ourselves now, it is all on us. We cannot blame the past for our future unless we allow the past to control our future.

So, starting today, we need to reclaim our lives and discard anything from our past that does not serve us in creating a happy today and tomorrow. We must quit judging ourselves. We need to either accept who we are or change what we do not like. But we need to do it for us and us alone.

"Accept everything about yourself — I mean everything, You are you and that is the beginning and the end — no apologies, no regrets."

- Clark Moustakas

Now, once we have either accepted us for us or are making the changes that we feel we need to make then we can also stop judging others and accept them for who they are. You see, when we judge others we are only pointing out things we really do not like about ourselves for people are simply a mirror unto us! So, if we are OK with ourselves, then we can be OK with others!

Acceptance allows us to look past our differences and find common ground on which to meet. It enhances communication because we are not spending our precious energy judging but rather openly engaging with others. Acceptance pushes away our fears for we are not afraid of what we accept. It allows us to be fully alive for we greet everyone and everything with an open heart and open mind. It shows us that we are truly more alike than different. It allows us to truly live in the moment with the carefree outlook of a child.

"Happiness can exist only in acceptance."

- Denis De Rougamont

Tolerance

"Tolerance and celebration of individual differences is the fire that fuels lasting love."

- Tom Hannah

What is the difference between acceptance and tolerance? Acceptance helps us to find common ground and the similarities we have with one another. Tolerance allows us to recognize the differences and accept them as well.

People with rare sense recognize both the similarities and differences in all of us and understand that is what makes us unique.

So, in essence we recognize the whole person and celebrate each other, for who we are, not who we wish them to be.

"It makes no difference as to the name of the God, since love is the real God of all the world.."

- Apache Proverb

Tolerance is what the founding fathers had in mind when they created the framework for the United States by allowing for personal expression through freedom of speech and freedom of religion. When we show tolerance we are living in spirit for again there can be no judging if we are truly tolerant of others.

Tolerance also exposes and destroys ignorance, for the more we learn about the differences we possess the more tolerant we become of one another. For even in our differences we will find common ground. Take religion for an example. If we truly take the time to learn the teachings of all the major religions we will find they are all based in love.

Just by learning we cast away fear and doubt and replace ignorance with knowledge. In doing so, we cannot be influenced by those who would use fear to keep us separate from one another. They cannot use fear for we are not afraid of the known but rather the unknown. Once we know the truth, fear and doubt can no longer control us!

If we want the world to change for the better then we have to become more accepting and more tolerant. The world is a mirror for our thoughts. If our thoughts come from fear, we will get things that frighten us. We have to find where we are the same and where we are different and then take the time to learn the truth about one another.

And we have to start inside of us! When we become more accepting and tolerant of ourselves we can then begin to do the same outside of ourselves. It is through finding the truth that will truly and finally be free of all the fear and doubt we have and begin to create a better world and a more promising future.

We are all in this together and the more together we become the more we can, as it is said, create heaven on earth. For being accepting and tolerant is another part of loving and when we love we create a world full of love. Ignorance, hate, fear and doubt cannot live in this type of world for the light of love replaces the darkness!

The highest result of education is tolerance.

- Helen Keller

JOURNAL AREA:

_____

_____

_____

_____

_____

_____

_____

_____

_____

_____

_____

_____

_____

_____

_____

Chapter 16: **Passion**

"Man is to be found in reason, God in the passions." - Georg C. Lichtenberg

When working on what the final chapter should be I decided that it should be about passion. People with rare sense live their lives with passion for we know that passion is the driving force of life. It is the fuel that drives the engine. It is the elixir of life.

If we do not have passion in our lives, we are simply going through the motions and that is not living at all. We were not put on this earth to simply take up space and air, each of us has talents unique to ourselves and we are truly living when we enthusiastically share those talents with the world.

We can not help but to be excited about life if we are full of passion. We can not help but to be full of energy if we have passion. We will only accept working in a job we love if we are working on what we are passionate about. The funny thing is if we work from our passions it will not be work at all for passion makes it exhilarating to be alive.

"Passion is in all great searches and is necessary to all creative endeavors."

- Eugene W. Smith

The challenges in our lives will not be insurmountable if we have passion. When we live a life of passion, we will see possibilities where once we saw only obstacles. When we are passionate and clear about what we want to do with our lives, doors will automatically open to us. The universe works on energy and passion is like nuclear fuel, powerful and renewable. We will work harder, play more, share more and love deeper. Our whole view of the world and its inhabitants will change when we live a life of passion. Living from passion is what people with rare sense do because we know that it is the only way to truly live.

In my case, my passion has always been about helping others. From the time I was in high school my classmates sought me out to help them solve their problems, especially with relationships. It was something I carried into adulthood and love to do even today. I love helping others become the highest and best they can be, which in turn actually helps me become a better person.

I found my passion early on in life and I lived it everyday in the jobs I had. However, there was a time very recently when I stopped working on what I was passionate about and changed careers. It does not matter what career it was, it simply did not fulfill my passions. We can be passionate about any job, it is an individual thing.

It turned out that my life became less rewarding and I was miserable. I was trying to fit into a career for all the wrong reasons and I knew it. I was even unable to write because I just could not find the words. When I was working from my passions the words simply flowed and once I turned off my passion it was like I was disconnected from the universe. The passion slowly drained from my life. I thought I would be helping others but it just did not turn out that way. The focus of this career turned out to be more money oriented than helping others.

Do not get me wrong, making money is good but helping others is good also and that was missing. I knew there had to be a way to combine my passion with making money and so I did a lot of introspection and reading. Two books that I highly recommend for this process are The Passion Test by Janet & Chris Attwood and The Millionaire Mind by T. Harv Eker. It felt that I was simply chasing money and not focusing on helping others and now I know I can have and do both.

Now that I am back on track, I have actually been able to write the last few chapters of this book and the passion is back. That is one beautiful thing about passion. It never really goes away; you just have to tap into it. I have once again and now I can live my passions by finishing this book and getting on with helping others. Tap into passion and you tap into the universe.

> **"There is no end. There is no beginning.
> There is only the infinite passion of life."**
>
> *- Frederico Fellini*

JOURNAL AREA:

_____

_____

_____

_____

_____

_____

_____

_____

_____

_____

_____

_____

_____

_____

_____

_____

CONCLUSION

Through our thoughts, words and deeds we create our world and our experiences of this lifetime. We chose it before we came to this earth plane and we continue to exercise our free will forever. Life is not the beginning and death the ending for there is no beginning or ending. We are eternal, forever, unending. We are in control and as much as we humans would like to blame others when things do not go the way we had hoped, we are surely only blaming ourselves, for we are all one.

We need to face each day knowing who we are and what we can do! We do not want to ever lose those child-like qualities of wonder and daring, qualities that allow us to continue to ask why and when we get an answer to probe even further, for we know that with every answer comes more questions.

We need to love with all our heart. We know that fear is an illusion. We need to continue to seek the answers and help as many of those we can along the way, for when we help others we most assuredly help ourselves. We need to be gentle with ourselves and other living creatures, including the earth. We need to replace hope and belief with knowing but understand that it is hope and belief that lead us to knowing. We must approach everything from a position of love for love conquers all and is one of the few constants in the universe. And we need to do it all with passion, the nuclear fuel of the universe. Finally we need to embrace change for that is what life is all about!

As I began this book I said that I have a unique way of looking at the world. In the end after going through the process of writing this book I have discovered that my view is really not so unique for many others have written about the same things that I have, I guess I just am putting them in my own words.

There is one set of books that I believe we all should read, especially if we want to "ah ha" a lot. The Conversations with God series by Neale Donald Walsch are great for that and are indeed full of RARE SENSE.

I certainly hope this book has touched you in a special way. I realize that you may not agree with everything I had to say here but I believe it will get you to think and I know I am a better person for bringing it to you.

Love and light always!

Layout and Design by:

ISBN 142513341-X

9 781425 133412